# Simple Fantasies

*poems by*

# Sujash Purna

*Finishing Line Press*
Georgetown, Kentucky

# Simple Fantasies

*Dedicated to all our strange and wistful dreams*

## ACKNOWLEDGMENTS

Warmly thankful to the readers, the editors, and the publishers of the
following journals and
presses where some of these poems first appeared:

*Poetry Salzburg Review*—Breast Pocket
*Bengaluru Review*—The Brick Mahal by the Railroad; Alibis Do Not Work
When You're Young
*Moonstone Arts Center Press*—Scared of Water
*The Bombay Review*—Miriam; Clotilde; Green Genteel
*Missouri's Best Emerging Poets*—An Urn on a Bookshelf
*Sylvia Magazine*—Chalked Out
*decomP*—Curry Stains
*Plainsongs*—A Monologue of a Theater Teacher
*Finishing Line Press*—A Christmas Gift; Moments and Lapses
*Five 2 One*—Pelting Pouring
*Telepoem Booth*—Simple Fantasies; Light Layers Lapis Lazuli
*Poet's Haven*—Holding on to

Publisher: Leah Huete de Maines
Editor: Christen Kincaid
Cover Art: Jess in the Wine Woods: Ryan Labee (www.ohthatryan.com)
Author Photo: Roxanne Chong
Cover Design: Elizabeth Maines McCleavy

Order online: www.finishinglinepress.com
also available on amazon.com

Author inquiries and mail orders:
Finishing Line Press
PO Box 1626
Georgetown, Kentucky 40324
USA

# Table of Contents

*"In dreaming*
*we travel to a place where all is forgiven."*

—Hélène Cardona, *Dreaming My Animal Selves/Le Songe*
*de Mes Ames Animales*

*"I just want to go out*
*every night for a while"*

—AIR, *Cherry Blossom Girl*

## Breast Pocket

The shape of a pocket is a random dart
in the darkness of embroidery.
The rest of the men took their hands,
caroled all winter until the break.
Breast and the ribcage now echo back
and forth and unlike the farthingale
of Victorian England. Was it developed
a single drop on a snare drum,
handclaps for the gum, the adhesive—
stick my stitches, stick my stitches—
until the doctor comes? The embroidered
jewel made you smile, on a gurney,
back from the industrialized age.
Let go off the past and focus on
what random shapes make us
guess at the Fibonacci, dress like fobs.

## The Brick Mahal by the Railroad

There are mouths that feed words in the cells
that travel past the cardiac arrests
in an upstate swing motion, in Amtrak veins.

I am past the age I cannot walk past a red brick Mahal
without thinking there used to be people talking
inside; now it's all nests of birds. The roof fell in

in an old storm, long ago,
I wanted to to be a scientist someday,
so I could create a machine

that captures the noise
in the air, like vacuum cleaners,
the bags behind them shaking with weight
of our words,

as if you bagged stones of rubble;
the brick mahal's roof didn't fall for no reason;
you didn't learn the words for no reason;

our pages were grown out of fern in the night dew,
to catch the image of the abandoned house,
decayed and forlorn, crickets chirping,
beads of drops resting, cradled in folds of rust,
rubble and debris, broken pieces,
waiting words, patient patiently.

## Alibis Do Not Work When You're Young

Mood swings change the conversation.
The colors of beetles crawling out of the dark
tailing you to your sleep, they follow like lies.

Until the girl held in prison screams you up
awake in the dead of night, you're perspired,
yet the magnetic name tags won't fall.

When you clutch on to them as you squeeze
the past out to drain into the hole of no remembrance,
the turn of the screw will come to haunt you;

the teeth shaped words among the cluttering,
clasping, clearing of the venting caterpillars
that never will be born into butterflies,

into the light. The dead are supposed to fly
but they are stuck like alibis that never worked
against you, against me, or anyone else.

We pretended never to know the dark:
the coil of smoke comes out the metal,
breaks out see-through sifted through the pile.

## Scared of Water

There have been moments like effigies
made of hay and golf balls
that stare blankly at the inquisitive.
I happen to stare blankly at them too.

The other day I was drowning in a pool
of moments like these:
I was black-suited, red-tied, white-shirted
worn-shod, dementia-fevered,

like all the prolonged noise of -eds.
I was staggering in my answers
to a pair of towers of words and wisdom
lighthouses, Helios in the night.

I lowered myself too much
like a drunken sailor, ashamed of my poor skills
navigating my boat for answers.
I was scared of the water.

## Magnified Resemblance of a Love Song

I was told to write with details.
Here is my big shot at it with plunging words:

Dark blue glow of a sparrow on alabaster skin
as she holds up her shirt to show me
her timber of fair trunk, slender like ivy.
I could have heard her laugh from thousand miles
if she wasn't evanescent like the moment
I saw her sparrow.

She is delicate like the jewels
on the edges of her leaves, dew-soaked;
cold is a word I wouldn't use but alluringly cool.

She is maybe a fairy,
goes lost constantly in her steel-hot real world,
goes trapped in a barrack of her greenly
cylinders of gloom that free her, yet slave her;
she goes lost in bubbles and smokes,
she is the one with a glass-pin scraping dark rust,
she is a dreamer, unaware of my plunging words
magnifying her like a bug in an orb
echoing love songs.

## Miriam

She is a mystery
with her belly out on her bean bag.
She tells me:
*I got almost raped by the guy*
*I met at the orientation*
*and dated for a month or so*

I shouldn't have bent her fender
when I knew that the grocery bags
from Walmart would be awkwardly
staring at us, when we didn't have
anything more to say.

An intruder from the pages
of Truman Capote,
she allows other Miriams like her in my room
to haunt her and take her space,
to take her place;
they sit with me to paint with watercolors,
let out post break-up angst over coffee cups
full of pinot noir. I remember once

Miriam took a jumbo pitcher of sangria
from the bottom shelf,
breaking the residence rules of her dorm.
Watercolor paintings slept in around her shelves
full of dead writers and haiku books.
The tiny hearts around Basho's words
screaming her love that hides behind.

...

In Kansas City, they say, she is a great bar-
tender now, tending old folks with gray
Boulevard Pale Ale, sprinkling mustache.

Sparkled eyes see her glide underwater,
under a sea out from time and society:
She doesn't age after all these years.
Through the crystal rocks of ice
you can see she is
in your room after all these years
behind these words, Miriam.

## Chalked Out

A list of foods were made and sold,
or presented and left alone, cold.
The relieve of hunger at the sight
of the names of unforgivable taste:

Mississippi Mud River, the torrid,
the marinating mangoes in a jar,
the all-for-show keeps the tips,
coming into the steps, the staircase,
the neon green shirt, the sliding
sleuths of thousand island dressing
from the sandwich we shared.

People belching and bleating out
insignias in the shape of sharp
phrases to make a point.

Stella Artois in hand the husband
keeps an eye on his kids so they
don't burn this whole place down.
A cop asking for a couple of iced
coffees after a long night to trace
the location of a driveby gunshot.

There is a stopwatch somewhere
in this building that is counting
the time it took to get used
to a ceiling of an intricate design.

There are chalked out signs
loudly announcing the new creations
of drinks nobody heard of before.
And then there is one outside on the
sidewalk telling you when and where
a man was found dead.

## An Urn on a Bookshelf

We finally went to the coffee-shop
I thought was closed on a Monday morning.
With clocks stuck on the wall, we were bound by time.
Caffeine addiction for me was a sharp contrast
to her caffeine allergy, so I focused on her green eyes instead
and red lipstick.

There were ghosts from long lost past on a bright sunny day:
I didn't tell her I was scared of them.
So that it wouldn't scare her away.
Instead I took a deep breath and
counted my blessings
and those faintly outlined silhouettes lingered
and I tried to focus on the living, the leaving

green eyes and red lipstick.

She gave me her hand-sanitizer with a strawberry scent
and as I carefully poured a few drops on my palms, reflections
of her fingernails with light purple and dots of blue,
on spherical glob of watery domes
looked back at me, whispered,
with a faintly fading fragrance,
*Hold on to me now,*
*I am all you have*
in a whirlpool of distilled nothingness.

I was numbly surprised
She didn't just storm out of the shop
and join my band of ghosts,
no, not yet but soon.
Instead she told me her own ghost story:
*Jack*
*sitting on my bookshelf*
*in an urn*

## Clotilde

*I feel sick all day long from not being with you,*
*I just want to go out every night for a while* —AIR

Chesterfield cigarettes turn into Marlboro
for the pursuit of their American dream.
The two French girls
set up the only olfactory battle in the air
between the garam masala flavored chicken curry
and their French perfume.
They cook chicken curry in France too,
just the way I do.
Only they add sour cream in it. Says
the girl with the hardest-to-say name,
with a silver bracelet made back in Paris.

They tell me the French say cats and dogs are a cowboy's lasso,
when they talk about heavy rain in the land of Gaul.

The girl with the hardest name
and the silver bracelet eats
with her hands for the first time,
rice and chicken curry on her plate,
and as her jeweled fingers clasp
a cube or two maybe,
Renoir's love walks
out from the frame.

## Green Genteel

She wore green;
green lipstick,
green eyeliners lining green,
eyelashes deigning a mien,

quiet, a glass of water
in hand, she looks around
the room full of *bastards*
and *godly children.*

She decides not to judge
just as her water
genteel she keeps
in her green.

On St. Paddy's Day
she remembers him
then she leans in
forward and grins

at a selfish me.
*I am sorry but listen*
*I have to be in*
*the house by fifteen*

I will keep the water
I say.
I need to hydrate
I say.

She keeps herself still
and silent
just as if her water
and she

swapped
their skins.
A green genteel
both coloring.

## A Monologue of a Theater Teacher


I go and break the Proscenium fourth wall
almost every day after I have my 3 o'clock
Starbucks blonde roast, no sugar, no
creamer.
Students know me as I know them,
but only if they could realize the horror,
of knowing everyone by their first and last
name. I wouldn't be teaching this class,
I would be in every movie and TV show
reciting the names on the credits, but
then I would not sleep at night.

In a fighting scene there should be
only two people, give and take, act and
response,

but three people bring in all the confusion.

## Curry Stains

I knew how hot it would feel,
amidst the late August sweat beads,
across your décolletage, almost a
teeming mecca of pilgrims.

They were bowing and listening
to the breeze as if they were there
splashing watery gravy with basil
sprinkles, not knowing why.

I could see you an amidst these
dark green specks, floating
swimming against the current of time,
a golden rush of sunkissed goosebumps
across the nape, a thin strip of metal
laced like a thirsty dream for touch.

Your white dress got stains, turmeric
with olive oil as you tried
the hot steaming froth of what
I called a reason to have you over,
or perhaps an excuse, a buoy in a sea,
the orbs of the night's glistening eyes
in awe with you being there with me,
soluble almost two beings in one,
in this blissful moment of mixture.

## A Christmas Gift


I almost forced you to return to my memory
as if on a Ouija board, seeking a spirit. You came.
You were waiting outside the glass door
with letters from a world I have never been before.
I got distracted, a lavender smell of your hair,
I saw you standing outside, in your gray beanie-
trying to keep them from a fall to your neck;
city lights glint and a lure from neon signs.
The night skyline of a city we knew so little about almost made you
its queen, maybe just for the night, or maybe it took you away from me,
just then maybe, or just until dawn came to both of us.
We were inside a glass box of a shop by the monastery;

a drizzly drowsy man in a burnt orange wrap around his body
gave me a vacant look, as I paid him and snuck a mini Buddha
in the newspaper bag, hoping not to get caught by you.
You knew, waiting outside, I got it for you for Christmas,
and I knew that by the time Buddha came out of his wrapping,
you'd be leaving a long chemtrail on a December night sky.
No longer the crown holder of this night, you would be
thousands of miles apart, from this town, from this country,
from me.

## Moments and Lapses

My empty dorm room probably smells as same
as it did the day I arrived with my two maroon suitcases.
There was this big buzzing noise from the a/c
that rang in my ears like the plane engines of a 17-hour flight.

The empty dorm room three stories above
probably smells just the way it did when I followed her,
like a child, her hand holding mine, taking me up
to her bed, teaching me how to unhook her bra,

as we mixed Jack Daniels with Sprite, I pretended
I liked her favorite show, to show I liked her too.
The purple pillow probably smells the way
like it did the night we spent in that moon-lit room.

Four stories below those carpets on my way in
and back from work are only there to take me back
to the same smell I had to leave behind, a year ago
with two maroon suitcases and nothing else.

I remember moments and lapses, and ghosts buzzing
like bees on a honeycomb of gilded space and time.
an untrained astronaut right before the landing,
I look for the same spot, at a different time.

## Pelting Pouring


Rain, cats and dogs, rain,
I learned when to say what
or did I really?

I pelt my words with bad timings,
as if catapulting meteors
in some vast bald-headed sky.

Technicalities and good sounds
only in the wrong time
hurt me back in gravity.

I pledge myself to be the reservoir,
a tank of names, of actions,
of people, of feelings,

but there are certain choices
when a certain time like a red beeping noise
bursts in and I blank out

with pelting pouring
lack of words, filling in
cavities of quietude

gravity zooms in on me, landing
heavily, in droplets, in globs
rain, rain, cats and dogs.

## A Vampire Story

I knew it all along:

perfectly measured in a box of sand
is the treacle smeared with genuinity,
collapsing songs of potatoes and molasses
engineered to tickle the ears
beyond raspberries of laughter.

Old fools with superlatives,
like candies and strangers,
they walk hand in hand.
often in minivans to pick up
whoever wants to hear

a vampire story is the end
double-lives in peregrinations
adulterated flesh with soul
like punctured tires
trundle, roll, and then fall apart.

We are all part of it.

## A Time Traveler of a Realist Fiction

Drawn from a chestnut colored body of a four-legged physique
is a heart made of the wanderlust that travels, crossing zones
of time and space, and of reality and the imagination
that ditches us again and again till she makes her olive cheeks wet,
for she is the heart drawn and thrown in a time machine
that took her across time zones, a basket of bronze holding;
a mercurial litany barely kissing the walls, but only when in a box
of home with her chestnut gleam, she can nestle in, in her black socks,
black breeches, brown boots, brown hat and brown eyes,
a river of auburn mixing in, with an ocean of chestnut breeze,
back from a journey, she is a time-traveler from a real story.

## Simple Fantasies

I declare the clouds as serenading minstrels
with a November rain that sparks up an emotion
right before we stare at each other's eyes.
It rains, and we kiss.

Little rivulets of water down the roads
of our holding hands are just us
melting down from years behind us
washing down with a house of leaves.

I am no more haunted.
Their departure doesn't scare me,
with you beside me, we can cup our hands,
catch watercolor raindrops, and we kiss.

My fantasies are simple:
they start with our gazes locked,
then the fragrance of your breath
mixes with the smell of the rain,

then the watercolors draw us again;
God's Monet or van Gogh on earth at work
with you, with me, and the rest of the world
behind us, and we kiss.

## Light Layers Lapis Lazuli

Indignant indigo mix and embrace
the dark meteorite and the sunrise
beams echo through cornucopia.
Are they tears? No? Is it joy?
Aisles between the church benches
glowing in mid-October sun and hymns;
Yours are a pair with dreams,
of Love? Or the hope of touch?
Light layers lapis lazuli bathing
saturnia in your eyes.

## Holding on to

a place where the last
noise of the rustling wind went
came back never with
the dropped dead leaves,

not even the past month
could crawl in like sleepy
dreamy flowerbugs or a holocene.

Time runs away like rustling
leaves brushing gently
against our bare feet,
breaks in among the wavelengths
smiles while gently snoring
shoring against the green
or the grinning sun, aware
of our reveries.

Tie-dye shirts and Yellow
Submarine from the boom-box
cannot take me away
from the decorated letters
you worked on over the summer
hung below the table.
Your root-beer floats,
your psychology book, then
a pair of distant rainy domes
of bluely thatched homes
etched in the horizon
amidst these rustling winds
dead leaves. As if looking
through a rainy window
at a cornfield or in a drive-in screen.

I saw your blue eyes were
gazing back at me;
for a moment I thought I found my home,
in those paintings of dreams in paradigms
I saw the watercolor, in a never-dying fashion,
never drying around the shore
I kept holding on to

**Sujash Purna** is a Bangladeshi poet and photographer based in Madison, Wisconsin. A first-year PhD fellow at the University of Wisconsin-Madison, he is the author of *Biriyani* (Poet's Haven), *Azans for the Infidel* (Mouthfeel Press), and *Epidemic of Nostalgia* (Finishing Line Press). His poetry has appeared in *California State Poetry Quarterly, Reed Magazine, South Carolina Review, Hawai`i Pacific Review, Kansas City Voices, Poetry Salzburg Review, Gutter, Stonecoast Review*, and others. A 2022 Anaphora Residency Fellow and *Moon City Review* Creative Nonfiction Award Winner, Sujash is the poetry editor for *Pyre Magazine*. Sujash and his photography can be found on Instagram *@poeticnomadic*